NOTES TO SELF

Sonya Teclai

Dedicated to Aida Mansfield and Teclai Berhane.

Let people grow in peace.

I don't know what I'm looking for,
but I'll feel it when I find it.

Don't let attention fool you into
thinking it's respect.

No one said evolving was easy.

The best thing you can do is give people enough
room to feel free to be themselves.

Sonya Teclai

You can tell a lot about someone by the way they
react to not getting what they want.

You can't do the bare minimum and
expect to get what people give their all for.

Do not undermine the value of a clear
conscience . . . it can work wonders
for your health.

Sometimes you'll want more for someone than
they want for themselves.
Sometimes you'll want more from someone
than they're willing to give.

Sonya Teclai

I don't have to believe in it to understand it.
I don't have to believe in it to respect it.

Confidence can change your life.
Grow it. Own it. Exude it.

I am who I present myself to be . . . and however
people register that is not entirely up to me.

Go in the direction your soul pulls you in.

You can look at the same thing for years,
leave it behind, and experience something new.
Then come back and see that
same thing completely differently.

When it comes to love . . .
you'll know it when you feel it,
and you'll feel it when you know it.

If you have nothing nice to say,
then reevaluate your happiness.

I need what I need, I want what I want . . . and most of the time, the two get mixed up.

Trust is an ongoing battle between how much you earn versus how much you give versus how much the other person deserves.

Drama rarely follows people
who mind their business.

There are times when God speaks.
You might not hear the words, but you'll see.
You'll see.

Be you . . . whether they're looking or not.

Be careful where you look to fill those voids.

Knowing someone and knowing of
someone . . . they are two different things.

Loyalty, dignity, morals, good heart,
and good character. . .
this is the essence of humanity.

Caring too much about what people
think of you is useless.
Most people don't even know what they
think of themselves.

Be good to you. Be happy with you.
Be true to you.
That will reflect with others on its own.

Passion is a power in itself.

Good quality will attract the quantity.

One of the biggest mistakes we make is
assuming that other people think
the way we think.

Energy is valuable. Spend it where it's worthy.

Sonya Teclai

Let go of anything that is toxic to
your progression.

Watch how people treat their subordinates
versus their superiors . . .
that's where you'll find true character.

I trust you to be you. Nothing more or less.

We get so caught up in our struggles,
we forget to acknowledge our accomplishments.

Don't say too much around those
that say too much.

Do what's right for you, even if it means
breaking someone's heart . . .
including your own.

Do not mistake the body for the soul.
One you'll have forever, the other you'll let go.

We have the tendency of chasing thrills just to
fill the vacancies.

Some people will hurt you in attempt to
heal themselves.

I ask questions I may not want or like the
answers to because I fiend truth
more than comfort.

Struggle is, at times, inevitable.
Survival is, most times, a choice.

There are some people you've just got to love
from a distance.

Your absence is a presence in itself.

I've got to stop taking simple things for granted . . . like waking up this morning.

A righteous man is a gem.

You're responsible for your intentions.
I'm responsible for my interpretation of
your intentions.

I have an affinity for things that money
can't afford.

I've seen maturity evolve more through
experience than age.

Stress has the tendency to blind you from your blessings.

Keep people around who won't let you have your
way when you're wrong.

Most of the time, the opportunity is there . . .
we're just afraid to take the risk.

Respect is measured by character, not finances.

People are quick to take credit,
and slow to take responsibility.

Manners are underrated.

Speaking things into existence does nothing without solid work ethic and implementation.

The most unpleasant conversations
I've had were with people who thought
they knew everything.

The man with the most game
doesn't have to spit any.

Funny thing about the mind . . . it can trap and
free you at the same time.

No one owes you anything.
The world won't let you forget that.

Soulmates do exist.
They feel inexplicably good.

We're *all* chasing happiness.

I think it's beautiful that you're different . . .
without trying to be.

The art of disciplining your emotions.
The art of knowing when to fall back.
The art of not stressing over things
you can't change.

Money can't buy you loyalty.

The things I love will never amount to the
people I love.

I can only hold you accountable for your actions, no matter how good your intentions may be.

Trust no words and most vibes.

A man's ego is just as sensitive as a woman's
self-esteem.

How much is enough if I always want more?

Thou shall not judge, because thou has fucked
up before too.

Once it's too predictable, it's boring.

Don't underestimate the power of
encouragement.

You can't expect love to be perfect when
people aren't.

I like to be attentive to the things people
value . . . it tells you what you need to know
about them.

I submit to God. I commit to who/what I love. I
omit any hindrances. It's that simple.

Don't let your delivery kill your message.

You only front when you're afraid.

I have no interest if my heart isn't in it.

They'll try to point out your flaws because they
hate their own.

I mind my business. That's my peace of mind.

Reading is fundamental . . . whether it's books
or body language.

Find your chill . . . then embrace it, baby.

Don't feel entitled to things you don't deserve.

Sometimes things fall into place . . .
other times, you have to move them.

Sonya Teclai

You don't have to dim someone else's light for
yours to shine.

When you build organically, the substance is unmatched.

People will talk about you when you're
down and out, and people will talk
about you when you're successful.
You choose what matters to you.

Two of the hardest things to do in times of
adversity is to keep your character intact and
your spirit uplifted.

Smile, baby. You're alive. You've got options.

Never let your ego grow so big that you don't
check yourself anymore.

Sonya Teclai

Stop for a moment and be truly grateful for
what you have.

Trust is a dangerous thing to play with.

My happiness is my responsibility.

Miscommunication is usually the root/source of every issue.

Staying positive takes a lot of energy and work
at times, but it feels so damn good when you see
the fruits of that labor.

Reconstructing a conditioned mind takes
discipline and time.

My worth doesn't sit on a man's tongue.

So many things will try to change you before
you even find you.

Say what you want. Be direct, be precise,
and be assertive. Hope to get it,
but be prepared to hear the word "no."

AUTHOR BIO

Photo By
Gregory Alexander

Sonya Teclai is an Eritrean-American poet, singer, rapper and songwriter based in Los Angeles, California. Growing up between Washington D.C. to Northern California—from Sacramento to the Bay Area—she began writing poetry at the age of 12 and songwriting at the age of 14. Through music, she found her love for writing, poetry, and creative expression. Having spent 8 years in New York City and growing up with her blunt African family, Teclai's style of writing reflects her environments—raw, eloquent, and direct.

In 2011, she became a part of The Good Quote's Fameless family where her quotes began to be shared worldwide. *Notes To Self* is the first book Teclai has published. Explaining the book in her words, Teclai says,

"Notes To Self is a public dialogue between my conscience and me. I compiled these quotes together with hope that others could relate and may find some truth, courage, and solace in facing their day-to-day lives."